© The Opiate Books 2023
Cover art and design by: Dale Champlin
ISBN: 978-2-9588567-2-4

There is a child inside the night
there is a child's heart
There is an innocence in the noise
the innocence of art

Table of Contents

Foreword 1
I Love Paris 5
Paradise 6
The Well 7
Permutations 8
A Poem For the End of the Year 16
The Salami Asylum 17
Milk 18
Stars 20
Delirium 22
Essaouira 24
Step Through Fire 25
Cold Salt Waves 26
A Room in Winter 27
Madrigal 28
My Bowery Loft 29
Syracuse 31
Venice 32
One Road Back 33
Out in the Forest 34
Minotaur 35
Human Cities 36
The Silence 37
And Then I Gave It All Away 39
A Poem About Everything 41

Foreword

"At night I would climb the steps to the Sacré-Coeur, and I would watch Paris, that futile oasis, scintillating in the wilderness of space. I would weep, because it was so beautiful, and because it was so useless."

-Simone de Beauvoir

A recent TikTok trend (a phrase that will undoubtedly date this for what remains of future reading generations) has favored calling out all the ways in which Paris is overrated. The trend applauds "humorous" scenes of expectation versus reality in a low-brow bid to illuminate Paris syndrome. This being defined as "a sense of extreme disappointment exhibited by some individuals when visiting Paris, who feel that the city was not what they had expected." Thus, the onslaught of videos is a case in point of Paris' ongoing ability to polarize. Though, in the past, it seemed that the city was far more readily glamorized before the philistine mediums of the twenty-first century came to roost, and the tourists could cite false scripture for their virality.

As for Paris syndrome, one might as well call it "Mona Lisa syndrome" since most people also feel disappointed when they see the ultra-famous but ultimately "rinky-dink" Da Vinci painting in the flesh (so to speak). One will note that the most common type of visitor seen in front of this painting tends to be Asian. And yes, the Paris syndrome is most commonly attributed to Japanese and Chinese visitors who are more prone to experiencing a certain kind of culture shock. But maybe what's most shocking of all to any tourist, regardless of where they're from is that Paris does, indeed, exist in reality (or whatever the overlords would have us believe is reality).

And so, barring the fact that these videos embody every aspect of the stupidity typically found among the ones that go viral, the so-called revelation that Paris is often flooded with trash and rats and smells like "piss, cheese and armpits" (to quote the TikTok user who allegedly started it all) serves to emphasize the many ways in which Paris is, in fact, a "real" city. Not a magical dreamland where you'll catch Audrey Hepburn dancing in all-black at some smoky underground club (a.k.a. *cave*). Granted, you'll see your fair share of gamine ingenues at any given milieu.

Only this time, their "bohemian" dance is done solely for social media in lieu of the sheer pleasure of it. Maybe that's what's changed the nature of Paris more than anything. Sure, there were always annoying tourists and pseudointellectual wannabes (usually from America) bombarding it, but now, there's an even more distinct caliber of, shall we just say it, unworthy dregs inundating the town. *Au présent*, it's for the sake of speaking ill of it (anything for virality, right?).

But, in the past, those who were harsh on it also knew that it was the only place they could really exist. Or rather, get semi-acknowledged as beings beyond their job title. At least if they were artists. Especially expatriates (as Oscar Wilde phrased it, "They say that when good Americans die they go to Paris"). From Henry Miller, who said, "To know Paris is to know a great deal" to Friedrich Nietzsche, who insisted, "An artist has no home in Europe except in Paris," the visceral reactions to Paris are, in general, what still makes it so appealing to an artist. Particularly a writer.

For no writer wants to live somewhere so utterly "milquetoast" that it elicits no strong feeling or reaction at all. Leave that sort of place to Claude Monet, who was content to putz around in his Giverny gardens. And really, he only left Paris in the first place for the same reason as most: financial difficulties. Who knows what might have happened if he had been "flush" enough to remain? Maybe his paintings wouldn't be so safe—subject-wise.

Of course, the *éléphant* in the room is that Paris undeniably fosters those who would never be able to continue working in an artistic capacity anywhere else once they've done something that gets them cancelled (see: Woody Allen, Roman Polanski, Louis C.K., etc.). Before the phenomenon of "cancelling," however, permitting artists to continue working post-scandal was simply called "separating the artist from the art." Allowing people to just "be," as it were. While some would rightly bill that as a grotesque symptom of patriarchy, there are also times when it's so goddamn refreshing to see how little Paris/France gives a fuck about falling in line with the side of the world it once partially "owned" before the Louisiana Purchase. And yet, despite said area formerly being under French rule, it seems, alas, that New York is the jurisdiction most frequently compared to Paris. And yes, that city also makes a cameo (along with, divergently, Essaouira and Syracuse) among the poetry in this collection. For what's more cliché than a New Yorker fleeing to Paris (e.g., Carrie Bradshaw) or a Parisian fleeing to New York (e.g.—oh wait, no self-respecting Parisian would ever actually *live* in New York)?

Although often compared to NYC, which has the same trash and rodent problem, Paris is the exact opposite. Less a city obsessed with "the hustle"—even after Macron's determination to remake it into the most capitalistic and U.S.-oriented place it can be—it remains a rare beacon (fitting, considering that prison tower-y light atop the Eiffel) of artistic hope. A place that artists can still flock to in search of both inspiration and a tribe. Just steer clear of the TikTok'ing twats along the way.

Simone de Beauvoir certainly would have. Preferring instead more conventional twats like Jean-Paul Sartre. And as for her assessment of Paris, "so beautiful" and "so useless," perhaps the latter classification is a result of how much we've been indoctrinated by our capitalistic society to believe that art *is* useless (unless, of course, it makes money). Therefore, so is a city that nurtures it. Maybe that's the real reason Paris gets its intermittent bad rap. It's an anachronism in an era that defies any city not to conform to the full-stop capitalist agenda. What's more, it's not a "City of Light," so much as a City of Divisive Shades of Gray (punctuated by the frequent rain).

To guide us through those shades is Rufo Quintavalle, covering the gamut of rollercoaster-y, often contradictory emotions that arise from living in Paris (/living overall). And yes, even just visiting. Though the visitors' opinions hold less and less credibility with each video posted for the purpose of "viral content."

Perhaps, instead, they ought to heed Quintavalle when he urges, "Come and take my hand tonight/and walk with me in human cities." Regardless of its ruination by false, rosy depictions (which then result in Paris syndrome) and, presently, cartoonishly shitty ones, there is no city more human than Paris. Because it is both of those things: rosy and shitty.

Genna Rivieccio
Editor, The Opiate Books
Summer 2023

I Love Paris

I love Paris in the springtime
I love Paris then you fall

I love Paris when my blood is up
and the square root of nothing is nothing at all

I love Paris when a girl with a look
sits in a cafe with a little white book

I love Paris when some bearded jerk
stares at a laptop and calls it work

I love Paris and I'm feeling fine
coke for breakfast then some natural wine

I love Paris and I simply love art
if I buy enough it will make me smart

I love Paris and its musical feast
the worst will be first and the best will be least

I love Paris when the circus is in town
Swarovski piercings and a Lagerfeld gown

I love Paris when the yellow vests
do their weekly thing with the CRS

I love Paris when the bombs go off
I love it when the churches burn

I love Paris why oh why do I love Paris?
it tries to teach me and I never learn

Paradise

As I was busy doing good
   it turned out I was doing wrong
As I walked out one morning
    a ghost walked in and stole my song

From then on every word I spoke
   was shrouded in a mist of lies
I built an image of myself
    and turned my back on paradise

The Well

And so
you go back
to the well

not
because
you
want to
but
because
you thirst

character
they say is
fate

but today
I woke
in sunlight
trembling

ants
on the table
were eating
a wasp

I had
almost
gone

almost
to the end
of my
mistake

Permutations

i.

arsenic clouds,
carpet's fibrous
trace, hi-ho human
evil pops up

pass the six
of clubs; lager
brings out
anger in you

grace's silo
hums, trams
tension
purrs

a tendril
grows, turns
makes its own
sutra

catch me
if you can, she sings,
our age is foul
and devious

dawn's tepid chorus
washes light on tundra;
wedding of sun
and veils

day begins
on cursal heights
of Muzak, then
trills to dusk

pale mist;
crocus flattering
thought's
acre

snakeskins drop,
curl; hardening
to dust
and serifs

paper-thin
forms,
rust marked
iron cusp

water
in columns
takes flight,
pours

watch me
in your
face; I'm
yours

ii.

yes but
I am not
yet up, I cannot
return

mercurial songs
tell truth
in jags
or reruns

femur, fists;
bad bones
jut
in pallor

helpful pills,
alone
but still
among men

let us,
trials over,
quit harm,
love

petunias cover
burial plots,
recurring charms
of wet sun

stem's quick
flash
once burst
is candor

begun in
major stress,
burnt lips
and cortex

new trusting
days flow
west, shunting
dark to dew

Euclid, Sappho,
the fun
is above
us

her music,
chaos;
the tuning
all wrong

Wellbutrin
halo, hell's
dull climax:
hope

iii.

hot air,
bubbles
of calm
thick musk

normality
crumbles:
God's fanciful
zero

crops and
bitumen; corn
pays tribute
to man

slow train
rumbles
on flashing
thunder

somatic
rust-bled
roadkill; muted
boasts

no brain,
just demons
chasing
muse or magic

coral pink
curve:
mortality
rune

gonads:
minute
commas,
hirsute toads

foaming butter
on rabbit,
duck leg, boar
with cut lemons

or platitudes
drop painful
hellos, black
minutes of rain

slob grabbing
cute boys,
flaccid muscles:
coma

polar light,
curved road,
wishful
cenotaph

iv.

put off
this heavy
flummox, its
dreary fur

undo its nets
and turn
to life, far-flung
noises call

unlocking
fearful orbits,
wet cauls
of sin

buttons shine,
capfuls of
spilt metal
sun

burnt stories
that lust
told, little draughts
of spite

full of fire
and rum's
horrid
tears

stupor,
lies
and customized
harm

but now
children laugh
tonight, petals
curl

fun-loving
dew falls
upon
this year

utopic breath
spurts
fog in
feral puffs

supposing
we can
just stop
still, be

hurt's morbid
death pull
lost in
leaf

A Poem For the End of the Year

I saw the slenderest
crescent today, hung
between buildings
as light gave way
to dusk; the more
we know the less
we know, the mind
blown open, a cliff
edge then air, made
open again (the soul
that is) for business

The Salami Asylum

In the salami asylum
it's electrodes à gogo and Château d'Yquem
it's Thorazine spritzers, Betelgeuse
and a cardboard kidney dish of phlegm

In the salami asylum
there's a stick thin Austrian nurse
who spends her time reminding you
that things can always get worse

She takes away your power
and keeps it safe with your will
at the top of a crystalline tower
on a five-and-a-half inch windowsill

In the salami asylum
the inmates are all doing life
there's a donor who's friends with the owner
and got a cut rate for his wife

She protested at first when he sent her
but to see her you never would guess
she seems so happy I almost resent her
her childlike guilelessness

In the salami asylum
you'll revert to the mean or the norm
the food is the color of entropy
and the rooms are hermetically warm

In the salami asylum
everything is swell
Pfizer sponsors loneliness
and GlaxoSmithKline hell

Milk

I'm like the glass
in your Knifey Moloko
the cream in your coffee
the umlaut in your tea

I'm a rat in the attic
and the in-laws in slow-mo
I'm the milf who puts
the milk in Milwaukee

I had a dream but it
ended in Moloch
and besides I forgot it
at dawn

there was some kind of membrane
some kind of master
there was some kind of flag
or shroud that was torn

My head's tied up
in the winding sheet
my feet are off with Hafez
and the Queen of Hearts

my whole's an unlikely
unheimlich passage
of text reflected
in a cataract glass

Uncle's boiling hemlock
or hunting Dr. King
the drains are flush
with opiates

and the rivers run down
and into the lakes
and the lakes are lakes
of suffering

Make mine a pint
of malarkey
the aimlessness
at noon

make mine the light
that dances
on the back
of a silver spoon

Make mine a field
of malachite
make mine a
martial tune

then make me one
and whole again
but please don't come
too soon

Stars

Last night
we lay
and
watched

the stars

the bear
the hunter
the heavenly
city

when
we are
split
apart
like atoms

broken
by God
and in our
desolation
raw

night's
emptiness
opens
onto order

like
that room
you
return
to
sometimes
in dreams

high
rafters
and birds
and steps
beyond
the door

wooden
steps
that move
in the
wind
and
lead you
down
to the
garden

Delirium

Yes
the spirits
but
I have come
to think
that man's
delirium

not just
a part
of his
reality

but also
part
of life

the spiders
as present
to him
as his wife
or
the peach
tree out
the window

but also
truly there

a residue

or a piece
of other
time

like
a dirt
street
in a city
the developers
overlooked

we swim
with
the dolphins
and say
the world
is one

but
we are
one too
with
the termites
whose gut
turns
wood to stone

and one
with
the leaf
cutters
stripping
the hill
to feed
their
underground
fungus

Essaouira

I opened the window and listened to silence
the city as perfect as the moon on the sea

The wind said nothing then gently Essaouira
the purpose of freedom to make another free

Step Through Fire

Step through fire and step into the sun
step out through every hurtful thing
your tiny hands have done

Step out from each accusation
step from your careless mouth
walk through the season of plenty
and through the time of drought

Step through love and through regret
and under silent skies
open the doors of contagion
and open your shining eyes

Open your shining eyes my love
the worst has already gone
the night is in abeyance now
and in a while dawn

Cold Salt Waves

I want a God
of cold salt waves
varied and infinite
as the sand in dunes

a God of second
and of twenty second chances
a God of daylight
and of dawn's ecstatic dances

I want a God
who sits with me
and laughs
and stares in amazement
at the summer clouds

a God whose face
is flecked
like water in rain
with kisses

I want a God of want
who needs you to exist

capillary, osmotic God
who blindly moves
and moving fills
each human lack
with love

A Room in Winter

Because one night in a room in winter
you laughed and made light of a child's soul
may existence curse you now and forever
and may you never be made whole

Because you tried to kill I will not kill
because you tried to take life life
because you tried and tried to destroy
I will cry tonight and tomorrow cry for joy

Madrigal

And all the lies
and all the rest
will pass away
and leave you
stronger

they don't exist
and you still do
and every day
like a madrigal
the evening light
goes on, persists
and stays a little
longer

My Bowery Loft

Well here I am in my Bowery loft
start the day with a start-up
and end it with a Zoloft
there on the wall is a Damien Hirst
John Lennon's head and Yoko Ono's purse
when I open the window I can hear the sound
of Joey Ramone turning underground

Valerie Solanas went bananas
and pumped a hole in Warhol
now they're cutting up men
and women again
and the shop on the corner keeps a book on your soul

The Turks hate the Kurds
and the Kurds hate the Turks
and the Nation of Islam hates the Jews
all of the actors are out of work
and the poets are looking for points of views
consensual couplets and all that they mean is
a long mea culpa for my short white penis

I remember sluicing down the fucking canal
and out the vagina dentata
teeth marks like cogs on my fontanelle
I remember my mother's spinach frittata

I remember you in your floral dress
your legs, your sex and your bird's nest mess
the first time I saw you you were ten feet tall
the second time the two of us were bouncing off the wall

Your face was like Elysium, your cunt a well-thumbed book
I climbed inside like Alice to get a closer look
a head without the shoulders
a heart without a brain

two finely formed and perfect things
in a festival of pain

We stayed inside a week or two
and never saw the sun
the window opened onto hell
and Jesus was it fun

Syracuse

It dwells beneath
whatever it was
the sun said

in Syracuse
in a naked room
the TV set
the morphine

birds are singing
childhood songs

long windows
open on a late
summer lawn

and then your face
or something like it

something faint
embodied
in the air

I felt it
in the sky once
saw it once
in the day's
blue dawn

cotton sheets
and cooking smells
love's transfiguring
possible touch

turn to me
in a naked room

turn to me
like rainfall

Venice

You wore it as fat, I wore it as scars
we both liked Venice because we didn't like cars

You liked diazepam, I liked booze
we both liked carrying on so far we still had a little left to lose

You were into disco, I was into God
we wanted to get even but the world was busy getting odd

One Road Back

You turn
in your sleep
and kick me
hard
and your hair
moves over
my face
and eyes

there is
one road back
from beauty
through
darkness

it is almost
as long
as your lies

Out in the Forest

Out in the forest I opened my heart
all I had ever done was there
and I looked on it and felt no shame

Where is Abdennour, servant of light?
Where is the Christlike Lucifer?

Here in the forest the earth smells sweet
I will stay in this kingdom of water forever

Minotaur

She had seen too much and was tired
had seen the half-formed shapes of fear
had been at sea when the wind stopped
and a presence beneath the waves drew near

Had moved through rooms of anger
and hated the man with the knife
had walked without conviction
through her own and another's life

Had sat and watched the adults sheltering in the lie
trading their beatitude for a two-bit alibi
had lived through a cloudless summer waiting for the rain
waiting for the waters to wash her clean again

She had seen it all and stopped mid-flight
and left everything unsaid
and found like a seam of ore in night
one perfect golden thread

Human Cities

I have been down inside that place
beyond words where the words are born
have been through noise and through the void
and into the cavern beneath the sea

Come and take my hand tonight
and walk with me in human cities

The Silence

I live alone in heaven
alone inside my song
you can step inside this place tonight
but do not stay too long

The sun and the moon may kiss me
upon my borrowed bed
but the son of man has nowhere
for him to lay his head

The daughters of society
are calling in the street
but there is only one of them
that I will ever meet

The children of oblivion
are making all their noise
but I would not trade my solitude
for those pretty girls and boys

It is here inside the silence
that I will wait for you
and a voice within the silence
will show me what to do

Come to me in radiance
and find me on my knees
your eyes like the light of prophecy
streaming through the trees

Your lips have tasted sorrow
and so can never age
your laughter in the evening
is the poem on the page

So be with me when morning comes
and friends will come and go
I have forgotten who I am
your silence is my pillow

And Then I Gave It All Away

And then I gave it all away
the nights, the deaths, the dawns
I gave away my Ritalin
and my plastic crown of thorns

I gave away my air miles
and my patent leather shoes
I gave away my agency
and my deeply long-held views

I gave away conviction
I gave away my art
I gave away attachments
and the borders of my heart

I gave away forgiveness
turned my back on judgment too
I gave away security
gave up on me and you

I gave away the morning
I gave away the day
I went naked in my seriousness
and naked in my play

The hired help was naked
the waitstaff and the cooks
the trees were moving backwards
and eating up the books

I sat among the cedars
I sat there all alone
I put my own humanity
inside the cedar cone

The sky became my blanket
it held me in my sleep
I lay beneath the willow tree
and let the willow weep

A Poem About Everything

Everything has to start
somewhere but a poem
about everything should
not start anywhere per se
in medias res is better and
best of all is no place at
all a poem about every
thing has no truck with
hierarchy or diachronic
progression and makes
nonsense of the notion
of non sequitur after all
as soon as two things
follow each other they
sequence and segue and
apophenia is more than
just a pretty word poems
about everything do not
exist in the plural there
is only one poem about
everything in the same
way there is only one
everything however as
pages are right angled
and monitors like cars
imitating carriages are
likewise rectilinear any
poem including a poem
about everything has to
start some place or at
the very least begin up
there where it began at
the top of the page the
top of the morning in
America is summer in
Siam and if it wanted

to this could be about
classifications or an ode
to the empire of the sun
or where the sun never
sets but this is not that
kind of poem it is more
oblique in the way it has
of playing politics if it
plays at all often enough
skipping straight to the
sport pages and working
the paper back to front
like a rebirth or a near
death tunnel of light
comes in a multitude of
gradations probably an
infinitude if you want
to be nit-picky about it
but for our purposes
four will do off and on
of course and the two
between when a brick
wall out your window
turns to brief heaven
are you getting it now
how a poem about a
wall in sunlight is also
a poem about every
thing that went into
that wall the trilobites
the epochs the epoxy
but also about the sun
about which we think
we know a lot because
it is always knocking
around but in fact we
barely understand and
also about the looker

and about their his her
upstairs neighbors who
for all we know are also
looking at the wall we'll
never know and so you
see a poem about all
that sun wall looker(s)
is really a poem about
each and every kind
of everything if you
can only stop or zoom
out long or far enough
a poem about breakfast
is a poem about every
thing in as much as it
contains both satiety
and want and wiping
down your inner thigh
or packing a suitcase
or making the bed
or a scene is also about
everything while poems
about fifty-seven things
are not and poems
about one thing are
not even poems even
too much stasis but
poems about two or
more things are as long
as you are mindful to
include the spaces and
give each of the two
or three things (and
each of the spaces
between them) room

Rufo Quintavalle is a poet and an actor. His previous collections include *Shelf, Weather Derivatives, hhereenow* and *Dog, cock, ape and viper*. He is the lead actor in the experimental web series, *Coldhearts: a poetical*, and you can also see him in Mikhaël Hers' film, *Les passagers de la nuit*, which was in competition at the 2022 Berlin Film Festival.

www.ingramcontent.com/pod-product-compliance
Lightning Source LLC
LaVergne TN
LVHW032014070526
838202LV00059B/6455